Integrated Science

for the **Caribbean**

Gene Samuel

Advisors:

Shameem Narine, Nadine Victor-Ayers, Ishaq Mohammed, Sheldon Rivas

Workbook 2

updated

Collins

HarperCollins*Publishers* Ltd
The News Building
1 London Bridge Street
London SE1 9GF

HarperCollins *Publishers*
Macken House, 39/40 Mayor Street Upper,
Dublin 1, D01 C9W8, Ireland

This book is produced from independently certified FSC™
paper to ensure responsible forest management .
For more information visit: www.harpercollins.co.uk/green

Updated edition 2017

10 9 8 7 6

© HarperCollins*Publishers* Limited 2015, 2017

ISBN 978-0-00-826306-5

Collins® is a registered trademark of HarperCollins*Publishers* Limited.

www.collins.co.uk/caribbeanschools

A catalogue record for this book is available from the British Library.

Typeset by QBS Learning

Printed and bound in the UK using 100% Renewable Electricity at CPI Group (UK) Ltd

Author: Gene Samuel
Advisors: Shameem Narine, Nadine Victor-Ayers, Ishaq Mohammed, Sheldon Rivas
Illustrators: QBS Learning
Publisher: Elaine Higgleton
Commissioning Editor: Tom Hardy
Editor: Julianna Dunn
Project Manager: Alissa McWhinnie, QBS Learning
Proofreader: Niamh O'Carroll
Cover Design: Gordon MacGilp
Production: Rachel Weaver

Contents

1.1 and 1.2 Diet and health and Food groups

1 Define the term diet. _____

_____

[1]

2 What is the function of the digestive system? _____

_____

[1]

3 The foods we eat can be classified into three groups called GO foods, GROW foods and GLOW foods. Give two examples of each type.

a) GO _____

[1]

b) GROW _____

[1]

c) GLOW _____

[1]

4 Complete the sentences about the three food groups.

a) GO foods provide us with _____

[1]

b) GROW foods provide us with _____

[1]

c) GLOW foods provide us with _____

[1]

5 Our source of fibre comes from _____ foods.

[1]

1.3 A balanced diet

1 What is meant by a 'balanced diet'? _____

_____

[1]

2 Complete the following sentences.

a) Carbohydrates are referred to as _____ foods.

[1]

b) Proteins are commonly known as _____ foods.

[1]

3 How does fibre help in our diet? _____

_____

[1]

4 Indicate whether the following groups of foods are balanced or not by writing BALANCED or NOT BALANCED on the line below each group.

a) _____   b) _____

c) _____   d) _____

[4]

1.4 Diet, activity and age

1 Write TRUE or FALSE for each of the statements.

a) People eat the same amount each day. _____

b) A person's diet depends on their age. _____

c) A secretary's diet needs fewer calories than that of a farmer. _____

d) Growing children need more protein in their diet than adults do. _____

e) If someone is not very active, they do not need carbohydrates. _____

f) For a body to repair, protein is needed. _____

g) All healthy diets consist of over 2000 calories per day. _____

h) Newborn babies sleep most of the time, so they do not
need much nutrition. _____

i) Bedridden people need a diet that provides a great
amount of nutrition. _____

j) A lack of the required nutrition leads to malnutrition. _____

k) The heartbeat is automatic, so it is not affected by nutrition. _____

[11]

1.5 and 1.6　The digestive system

1 Use the clues below to complete the crossword puzzle about the digestive system.

Across

3. _____ is the undigested waste from the body.

5. Food is chewed in the _____.

9. _____ are obtained from the foods we eat.

10. Proteins are broken down to _____.

11. The _____ is the size of a fist.

13. _____ acid is produced by the stomach.

16. The first part of the small intestine is the _____.

17. Food absorption occurs in the _____ intestine.

18. _____ is the removal of undigested food from the body.

20. The _____ in digestive juices chemically break down food.

Down

1. The small intestine is about _____ metres long.
2. Another name for the oesophagus is the _____.
4. The food passes along the _____ canal.
6. The stomach walls are very _____.
7. Food is broken down in the _____ system.
8. The enzymes in saliva convert _____ to glucose.
12. _____ is from plant material.
14. _____ is absorbed in the large intestine.
15. _____ is the second part of the small intestine.
19. The _____ mechanically break down the food.

[10]

2 A diagram of the human teeth is shown below. Label the types of teeth indicated by arrows.

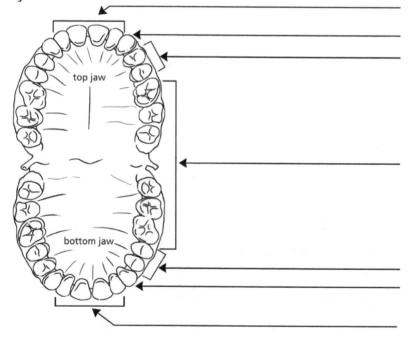

[4]

3 Complete the statements below.

a) There are _____ types of teeth in our mouth.

b) The _____ are for cutting.

c) The _____ are for tearing.

d) The _____ and _____ are for grinding.

[5]

4 Look at the diagram of a skull and answer the questions.

a) The dentition below is that of a/an:

    i) herbivore   **ii)** carnivore   **iii)** omnivore

b) My reason for my answer to 4 a) is

_____

_____

_____

[2]

1.7 The process of digestion

1 Complete the sentences about digestion.

a) During physical digestion, food is broken down into smaller _____.

b) During chemical digestion, food is broken down into smaller _____.

c) Physical digestion occurs in the _____ and _____.

d) Chemical digestion occurs in the _____, _____

    and _____.

[7]

2 Complete the table to show the type of food that is chemically broken down by each enzyme.

ENZYME	FOOD
Carbohydrases	
Lipases	
Proteases	

[3]

3 Circle the number showing the correct answer.

a) What allows the small intestine to have a large surface for absorption?

    i) a rich blood supply   **ii)** thin walls

    iii) numerous villi   **iv)** tiny capillaries

b) Nutrients in the ileum are absorbed into the:

i) bile   ii) blood stream

iii) thin walls   iv) digestive juices

c) The process of breaking large insoluble molecules into smaller molecules is called:

i) digestion   ii) ingestion   iii) absorption   iv) egestion

d) When food is chewed, it undergoes:

i) absorption   ii) chemical digestion

iii) physical digestion   iv) egestion

e) All of these substances contain potential energy, which can be released by digestion, except for one. Which one?

i) glucose   ii) sodium chloride   iii) milk   iv) egg

f) Peristalsis, or the squeezing of food through the digestive system, is an example of:

i) physical change   ii) chemical change

iii) digestive change   iv) ingestive change

[6]

1.8 and 1.9   Food structure and Food tests

1 Write TRUE or FALSE for each statement.

	STATEMENT	TRUE/FALSE
1.	When an egg is fried, the protein in the egg is denatured.	
2.	Some fats we eat are digested in the mouth.	
3.	Amino acids from protein are used to build new proteins.	
4.	Foods containing starch include rice, bread and macaroni.	

5.	Sucrose is easily absorbed into the body.	
6.	The human body cannot directly absorb animal protein.	
7.	Sugar molecules are broken down to sucrose for absorption.	
8.	The structure of animal protein is similar to human protein.	
9.	Fat molecules consist of fatty acids and glycerol.	
10.	Some fat is used as energy.	
11.	Fats are needed by the body to build cell membranes.	
12.	Any unused fat is passed out of the body as faeces.	

[12]

2 Why is it necessary to carry out food tests? _____

_____

[1]

3 Simple sugars and starch are both categorised as _____

_____

[1]

4 Using linking lines, match each food with its testing solution and the resulting change.

TESTING SOLUTION	FOOD	CHANGE
Benedict's reagent	Starch	Emulsify
Iodine	Simple sugar	Brick red
Ethanol	Protein	Blue black
Biuret reagent	Fat	Blue to purple

[4]

5 You would like to find out whether a food sample contains fat but you do not have the testing solution. Describe what you would do and the positive result you would get if the sample contains fat.

_____

_____

_____

_____

_____

[3]

1.10   Energy values in food

1 What information does the calorific value of food give? _____

_____

[1]

2 Below is the menu of food available at a breakfast bar. The calorific value of each item is shown.

FOOD	SERVING	CALORIES
Bagel	85 g	216
Biscuit	15 g	74
Scone	70 g	225
Slice of bread	12.2 g	28
Cornflakes	45 g	167
2 Weetabix	37.5 g	129
Sausage	60 g	151
Rasher of bacon	25 g	64

FOOD	SERVING	CALORIES
Butter	10 g	74
Cheese	40 g	172
Slice of ham	30 g	35
Mayonnaise	11 g	33
Can of coke	330 ml	139
Glass of juice	200 ml	88
Cup of coffee	220 ml	15.4
Milk	100 ml	66

a) Two friends are at the breakfast bar. Their choice of food is shown below. Refer to the values in the menu and give the number of calories each consumed that morning.

LIANNE'S BREAKFAST			KERRI'S BREAKFAST		
FOOD	**SERVING**	**CALORIES**	**FOOD**	**SERVING**	**CALORIES**
Bagel	1		Biscuit	2	
Cornflakes	2		Butter	1	
Sausage	2		Scone	1	
Cheese	1		Mayonnaise	1	
Milk	1		Slice of ham	2	
Glass of juice	1		Cup of coffee	1	
TOTAL	8		TOTAL	8	

[6]

b) Use the menu above to create a breakfast for yourself. Write it into the blank table below.

FOOD	SERVING	CALORIES

i) Your total calorie count is _____

[3]

ii) Explain why you chose any TWO of the foods you did.

_____

_____

[2]

1.11 Body mass index

1 What does the body mass index (BMI) of someone indicate? _____

_____

[1]

2 How would you know that a person is underweight?_____

_____

[1]

3 To calculate a person's BMI, you should divide their weight in kilograms by their height in metres squared. You will need a calculator. Complete this example.

Daniel weighs 56.8 kg and he has a height of 1.68 m. Find his BMI.

$56.8 \div (1.68)^2 =$ _____

[1]

4 In the ovals below, enter the information that will help you find your BMI.

My name: _____

$\div$ _____ ^{2} = _____

[3]

1.12 and 1.13   Weight gain and loss and Fat or thin?

1 Why does a person gain weight? _____

_____

[1]

2 Which type of food or food group is most responsible for weight gain? _____

_____

[1]

3 Name THREE places on the body where fat is easily stored.

a) _____

b) _____

c) _____

[3]

4 What causes a person to be obese? _____

_____

[1]

5 Why do less active people need to reduce their calorie intake? _____

_____

[1]

6 Write THREE factors that should be considered when someone decides to change their calorie intake.

a) _____

b) _____

c) _____

[3]

7 How does exercise help with weight loss? _____

_____

_____

[1]

8 Name THREE factors that may contribute to a person's size.

a) _____

b) _____

c) _____

[3]

9 Vera is obese and though she has been exercising and eating much less for the past three months, she is not able to lose any weight. What could be an explanation for her situation?

_____

_____

[2]

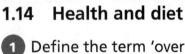

1.14   Health and diet

1 Define the term 'overweight'. _____

_____

[1]

2 The following diseases are associated with being overweight. Write sentences to show what each one means.

a) heart disease _____

_____

[1]

b) high blood pressure _____

_____

[1]

c) stroke _____

_____

[1]

d) type 2 diabetes _____

_____

[1]

3 Complete the sentences with the words shown below. Each word is used once only.

SHIFT   USED   OVERWEIGHT   REGULAR   BAD

a) It is important to have a _____ eating pattern.

b) It is difficult for _____ workers to keep to a normal eating pattern.

c) The body gets _____ to our eating pattern.

d) Changing eating patterns is _____ for the body.

e) Irregular eating patterns can lead to becoming _____ .

[5]

2.2 Structure of the circulatory system

1 What is the function of the circulatory system? _____

_____

[1]

2 The central component of the circulatory system is the _____.

[1]

3 Why is oxygenated blood pumped at high pressure? _____

_____

[1]

4 Use the diagram of the circulatory system to find the correct order for the sentences in the table.

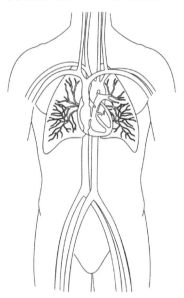

	BLOOD CIRCULATION	ORDER
a)	Blood is pumped from the right side of the heart to the lungs.	1st
b)	The blood returns to the right side of the heart.	_____
c)	In the lungs the blood receives a fresh supply of oxygen.	_____
d)	The blood returns to the left side of the heart.	_____
e)	The blood is then pumped to the organs of the body.	_____

[3]

5 Circle the best answer.

a) As it circulates, the blood provides your body with all of these, except for one. Which one?

i) oxygen   ii) nutrients

iii) a way to get rid of waste   iv) a sense of pain

b) These are vessels that carry blood back to the heart.

   i) arteries   **ii)** veins   **iii)** bloodlines   **iv)** valves

[2]

2.3 The heart

1 Write whether the following statements are TRUE or FALSE.

a) The parts that act like doors and control blood flow are called valves.

_____

b) The heartbeat occurs because the blood is travelling in opposite directions.

_____

c) Both oxygenated and deoxygenated blood flow to the heart.

_____

d) Heart muscles do not get tired.

_____

e) The septum allows free blood flow across the sides of the heart.

_____

f) The heart can live outside the body.

_____

[6]

2 Look at the diagram of a heart.

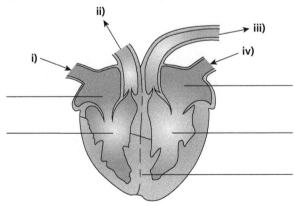

a) Name the parts of the heart indicated by the labelling lines.   [5]

b) Draw arrows on the diagram to indicate the direction of blood flow.   [2]

c) For each arrow on the diagram, write where the blood is coming from or where it is going to from the heart.

i) _____

ii) _____

iii) _____

iv) _____

[4]

2.4   Arteries, veins and capillaries

1 Give TWO features of each of the following:

a) arteries _____

_____

b) veins _____

_____

c) capillaries _____

_____

[3]

2 Write whether the following statements are TRUE or FALSE.

a) The inner diameter of arteries is small because the walls are very thick.   _____

b) Diffusion through capillary walls is easy because capillaries are one cell thick.   _____

c) After diffusion occurs, the capillaries die and are dissolved into the bloodstream.   _____

d) Venules join and connect to veins.   _____

e) All arteries carry blood to the heart.   _____

[5]

3 Each circle below represents the cross-section of a blood vessel.

artery   vein

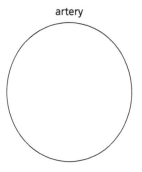 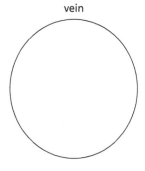

a) Draw the inner walls for each vessel to show the difference between an artery and a vein.

b) Say which of these blood vessels contain valves. Explain what these valves do and why they are needed.

_____

_____

_____

_____

[6]

2.5 Components of the blood

1 Name FOUR components of blood.

a) _____ b) _____

c) _____ d) _____

[4]

2 The table contains information about red and white blood cells. Write RED or WHITE in each row of the right-hand column to indicate which blood cell is written about.

	INFORMATION	RED or WHITE blood cells
a)	_____ fight any infection that might enter the body.	
b)	_____ contain a pigment called haemoglobin.	
c)	_____ transport oxygen around the body.	
d)	_____ may be phagocytes and lymphocytes.	
e)	A shortage of _____ causes a condition called anaemia.	
f)	_____ enclose germs into the cell and kill and digest them.	

[6]

3 Circle the correct answer.

a) Which is true about human blood?

i) The blood of all normal humans contains red and white cells as well as platelets and plasma.

ii) Some ethnic groups are unable to produce plasma.

iii) It is normal to have a higher proportion of white blood cells than red blood cells.

iv) All of the above are true.

b) The almost-clear liquid in which the cells travel is called:

i) lipid   ii) glucose solution   iii) plasma   iv) antibodies

c) The component of normal human blood which has the largest volume is:

i) red cells   ii) white cells
iii) haemoglobin   iv) plasma

[3]

4 Circle the correct answer in the right-hand column.

a)	Which of the following allows cells to get nutrients?	oxygen carbon dioxide blood other cells
b)	Our circulatory system soldiers are...	lungs white blood cells valves red blood cells
c)	Oxygen is important to both the blood and the cells because it...	helps in clotting carries nutrients is used to release energy releases white blood cells
d)	Blood from the lungs is bright red because it contains...	oxygen red lung pigment colourless carbon dioxide nutrients
e)	If someone has a large wound and blood that does not clot easily he or she may...	have to take doses of vitamins bleed to death be protected by blood soldiers suffer a heart attack
f)	The function of the arteries, veins and capillaries is to...	pump blood to and from the heart filter impurities from the blood transport blood to and from all parts of the body carry messages to the brain quickly

[6]

5 Write whether the statements are TRUE or FALSE.

a) Urea is transported by the blood to the kidneys. _____

b) Pulmonary veins carry blood that is rich in carbon dioxide. _____

c) The waste product of respiration is oxygen. _____

d) Urine contains the waste product urea. _____

e) Hormones are carried via the bloodstream. _____

f) Adrenalin is released into the blood only when we are afraid. _____

[6]

2.6 Pulse rate

1 Complete these sentences.

a) Pulses are caused when the heart _____ .

b) The pulse rate is the _____ of heartbeats to every

_____ .

c) The place in the body most commonly used to feel for the pulse is

_____ .

d) The pulse rate decreases as people get _____ .

e) An adult's normal heart rate is from 60 to _____ beats per minute.

[6]

2 Write whether the statements are TRUE or FALSE.

a) Physical activity can work against the harmful effects of
high blood pressure.   _____

b) To get health benefits, exercising must be vigorous.   _____

c) Heredity has effects on the wellbeing of your heart.   _____

d) High impact exercise is known as aerobic activity.   _____

e) Physical activity can prevent heart disease.   _____

f) The radial pulse is found in the neck area.   _____

[6]

2.7   Effect of exercise on pulse rate

1 Examine the graph below, which shows the heart rates of Darryll (▲) and Mikey (■) during exercise. Then answer the questions.

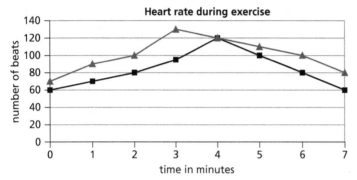

a) Who has the higher heart rate after two minutes? _____

b) After how many minutes were the rates furthest apart? _____

c) At what time did the two boys have the same rate? _____

d) How long did it take for each one to reach his highest rate?
   i) Darryll _____   **ii)** Mikey _____

e) What is the difference between the highest and lowest heart rate for each boy?

   i) Darryll _____   **ii)** Mikey _____

[7]

2 Carry out your own exercise experiment together with your group members or with one friend. Compare the differences and similarities by plotting line graphs on graph paper.

[3]

2.8 Health and the circulatory system

1 Name TWO diseases that negatively affect the circulatory system.

a) _____ b) _____

[2]

2 Give FOUR factors that contribute to diseases of the circulatory system.

a) _____ b) _____

c) _____ d) _____

[2]

3 Write TRUE or FALSE for each of the following.

	STATEMENT	TRUE/FALSE
a)	During a heart attack, the heartbeat goes to zero.	
b)	Heart attacks kill more men than women.	
c)	High cholesterol arises from many factors.	
d)	By reducing your salt intake you can reduce risks to your heart.	
e)	Low doses of aspirin can help to prevent another heart attack.	
f)	Obesity is the biggest cause of heart disease.	
g)	Heart disease kills more women than breast cancer.	
h)	To protect your heart, eat only fat-free foods.	
i)	Red wine can lower your chances of heart disease.	
j)	For a healthy heart, eat fish at least twice weekly.	
k)	Varicose veins occur when the valves in the leg veins stop working.	
l)	A non-smoker cannot get high blood pressure.	

[12]

3.2 Structure of the respiratory system

1 What is the function of the respiratory system? _____

_____

[1]

2 Label the parts of the respiratory system indicated on the diagram.

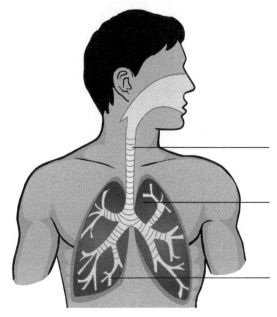

[6]

3 Circle the correct answer.

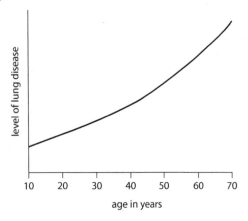

age in years

a) Look at the graph above. Which age group is most prone to lung diseases?

i) 17–20   ii) 25–40   iii) 50–70

b) From birth to age 30 the capacity of the lungs:

    i) remains unchanged   **ii)** increases   **iii)** decreases

c) After age 30 the capacity of the lungs:

    i) decreases   **ii)** remains unchanged   **iii)** increases

[3]

4 Where are the alveoli located? _____

[1]

5 What is the function of the alveoli? _____

_____

[1]

6 Match the sentence beginnings on the left with the endings on the right, so that the sentences are true.

a)	The exchange of gases in the alveoli takes place by…	a network of blood capillaries.
b)	The method by which air is exchanged in the body is…	diffusion.
c)	Each alveolus is supplied with…	different sizes.
d)	The walls of the alveoli are…	external respiration.
e)	The inner surface of the alveoli is…	subdivides into many bronchioles.
f)	The bronchus…	only one cell thick.

[7]

3.3   Gas exchange in the lungs

1 The diagram below shows an alveolus with a blood vessel. The four arrows, identified by labelling lines, show the direction of gases. Write which gas is represented by each arrow.

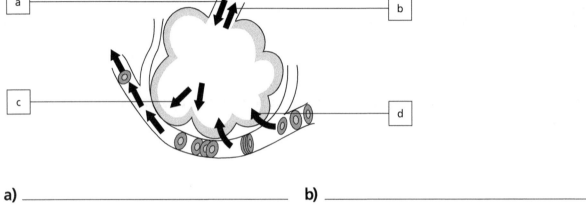

a) _____   b) _____

c) _____   d) _____

[4]

2 Circle the correct answer in the right-hand column.

a)	Which of the following is involved in gas exchange?	trachea bronchi	bronchioles alveoli
b)	Air going to the lungs travels through…	trachea and bronchioles nose and stomach	gullet and veins trachea and gullet
c)	Which of the following is needed for cellular respiration?	carbon dioxide oxygen	nitrogen hydrogen
d)	Which of the following is exhaled?	carbon dioxide oxygen	water vapour all of the above
e)	The blood vessels surrounding the alveoli are…	nerve endings veins	arteries capillaries
f)	Food releases energy in a process called…	ingestion respiration	digestion photosynthesis

[6]

3.4　How you breathe

1 Circle the correct answer.

a) The muscle that allows you to breathe in and out is the:

    i) trachea　　　　**ii)** diaphragm　　　　**iii)** tongue　　　　**iv)** stomach

b) Air enters your lungs through the:

    i) trachea　　　　**ii)** oesophagus　　　　**iii)** alveoli　　　　**iv)** vena cava

c) The bronchial tubes are:

    i) air passages inside your lungs　　　　**ii)** blood vessels inside your body

    iii) tiny air sacs delivering oxygen to the blood　　　　**iv)** connections between the air sacs and nerves

d) When you breathe in, the diaphragm _____ and the ribcage _____ .

    i) expands / contracts　　　　**ii)** contracts / expands

    iii) contracts / contracts　　　　**iv)** expands / expands

[4]

2 Write whether the statements are TRUE or FALSE.

	STATEMENT	TRUE/FALSE
a)	The ribcage protects the lungs.	
b)	Inhalation occurs when the diaphragm relaxes.	
c)	We breathe faster when exercising because the blood tells the lungs to work harder.	
d)	Inhalation is breathing in and out.	
e)	The brain controls the amount of air we breathe.	
f)	Normally, we can hold our breath for 30 seconds.	
g)	Both lungs are the same size.	
h)	As we sleep, the air we exhale could be enough to fill a bedroom.	

[8]

3.5 Respiration in cells

1 Use the clues below to complete the crossword puzzle about respiration.

Across

3. During _____ respiration, oxygen and carbon dioxide are interchanged.
6. Oxygen reacts with it to produce energy.
7. Carbon dioxide is a _____ product of respiration.
11. During _____ respiration, energy is produced.
12. Water and carbon dioxide are produced in the _____.
13. Water and carbon dioxide are carried to the lungs by the _____.
14. Excess water is lost from the body in _____.
15. The powerhouses of the cell.

Down

1. The movement of the lungs.
2. One way water leaves the body.
4. The source of energy in the body.
5. The _____ is an involuntary muscle.
7. A bi-product of respiration.
8. Internal respiration is also called _____ respiration.
9. The skeletal _____ are voluntary.
10. They have different concentrations of mitochondria.

[8]

3.6 Breathing rate

1 What does the breathing rate indicate? _____

_____

[1]

2 The following graph shows the breathing rate of Ishtaq as he sleeps and while awake, walking, jogging and running, each for one minute. Use the graph to answer the questions below.

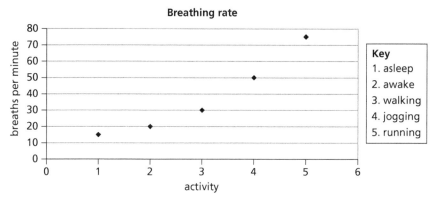

Breathing rate

Key
1. asleep
2. awake
3. walking
4. jogging
5. running

a) What is the difference between the number of breaths for sleep and running?

_____

[1]

b) Between which two adjacent activities was there:

  i)   the smallest difference? _____

[1]

  ii) the greatest difference? _____

[1]

c) Which activity had twice the number of breaths as another? _____

_____

[1]

d) Suggest what number of breaths may have been recorded if Ishtaq:

  i)   walked quickly _____

[1]

  ii) were afraid _____

[1]

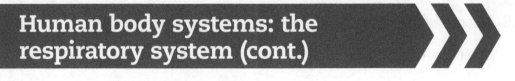

3.7 Exercise and breathing rate

1 The following graph shows the breathing rates of Rose, Grace and Asha as they sleep and while walking, happy and afraid, each for one minute. Use the graph to answer the questions below.

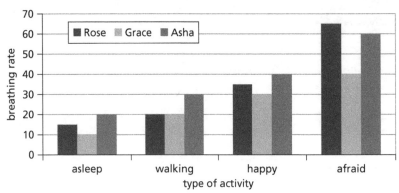

a) Which girl shows a constant increase in breathing rate from one state to the next? _____

[1]

b) What is the change in breathing rate between sleep and fear for each girl?

i) Rose _____ ii) Grace _____

iii) Asha _____ [3]

c) Place the girls in order from lowest increase in breathing rate to the highest increase.

_____, _____, _____ [1]

d) i) In which activity did two girls have the same breathing rate?

_____ [1]

ii) Write the names of the two girls who had that same breathing rate.

_____ [1]

e) i) Which girl breathes twice as fast when she is fearful than when she is walking?

_____ [1]

ii) For the girl in **e) i)** above, what is the ratio of her breathing rate when she is sleeping to her breathing rate when she is happy?

_____

_____ [1]

f) With which girl can you compare yourself? Why? _____

_____

_____ [1]

3.8 The effects of smoking

1 Name TWO harmful substances contained in cigarette smoke.

a) _____ b) _____ [2]

2 How does smoking affect the circulatory system? _____

_____

_____

_____ [1]

3 What does the disease emphysema do to the alveoli? _____

_____ [1]

4 What effect does emphysema have on a person? _____

_____ [1]

5 As well as diseases caused by smoking, there are many other diseases of the respiratory system. Find the respiratory diseases defined below in the wordsearch.

Search for the words that are written in CAPITAL letters only.

B	S	V	H	E	D	E	M	A	J	T	M	Y	M	O
B	S	I	S	O	T	S	E	B	S	A	C	Y	Z	B
H	T	B	S	V	R	Q	E	K	E	Y	A	S	L	S
R	S	R	C	O	L	M	K	M	Z	G	P	L	F	T
I	N	O	R	E	L	N	S	P	N	D	M	A	Z	R
A	H	N	D	M	A	U	H	U	M	A	O	S	C	U
Q	E	C	I	P	C	I	C	Q	X	C	E	T	I	C
A	E	H	S	H	R	F	N	R	B	U	G	H	T	T
Q	N	I	T	Y	H	E	I	O	E	E	F	M	S	I
M	B	T	R	S	Y	K	C	B	M	B	N	A	Y	V
K	B	I	E	E	O	A	N	N	R	U	U	M	C	E
O	D	S	S	M	X	U	L	H	A	O	E	T	R	Z
T	T	B	S	A	E	T	U	C	A	C	S	N	L	V
C	C	H	R	O	N	I	C	L	L	O	T	I	P	H
N	T	O	R	A	T	P	B	M	R	M	T	S	S	E

ASBESTOSIS: lung inflammation caused by asbestos

ASTHMA: inflamed airways

PNEUMONIA: bacterial infection of the alveoli

EDEMA: fluid in lungs

CANCER: rapid growth of abnormal cells

EMPHYSEMA: lung damage

CHRONIC bronchitis: persistent cough

TUBERCULOSIS: progressive pneumonia

ACUTE BRONCHITIS: sudden infection caused by a virus

CYSTIC FIBROSIS: accumulation of mucus

Chronic OBSTRUCTIVE pulmonary disease: inability to exhale properly

Acute respiratory DISTRESS syndrome: severe, sudden injury to the lungs caused by a serious illness

[7]

4.2 Physical properties of matter

1 What are physical properties? _____

_____

[1]

2 Physical properties may be classified as either QUALITATIVE or QUANTITATIVE. For each of the examples below, write whether it is qualitative or quantitative.

a) Water boils at 100 degrees Celsius. _____

b) Dry cereal is brittle and dull. _____

c) A black shirt will stain a white one during washing. _____

d) 150 g of sugar dissolves slowly in 2 litres of water. _____

e) Fresh food tastes delicious. _____

f) This type of material stretches more than the other. _____

[6]

3 Qualitative properties are observed with your _____.

[1]

4 Quantitative properties are measured by using _____.

[1]

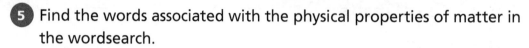

5 Find the words associated with the physical properties of matter in the wordsearch.

L	Q	C	X	M	Z	E	P	B	I
D	S	O	S	A	F	R	K	O	W
S	S	N	T	G	P	U	C	I	L
R	E	D	R	N	R	T	I	L	M
U	N	U	E	E	U	C	T	I	E
O	D	C	N	T	O	U	S	N	L
D	R	T	G	I	L	R	A	G	T
O	A	I	T	S	O	T	L	K	I
T	H	O	H	M	C	S	E	B	N
A	P	N	L	E	T	A	T	S	G

boiling
colour
conduction
elastic
hardness
magnetism
melting
odour
state
strength
structure

[6]

4.3 Chemical changes

1 How would you define a chemical property? _____

_____

[1]

2 Observe the illustration. The tablet, which effervesces in water, is placed in a jar of water.

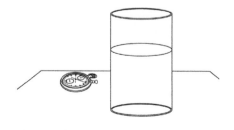

a) Give two reactions that you expect to occur.

   i) _____

   ii) _____

b) What does the effervescence indicate?

_____

[3]

3 Five new copper coins were placed in vinegar to oxidise for a few hours and were then compared with new copper coins not put in vinegar.

a) What colour are new copper coins? _____

b) What colour are copper coins that have been left in vinegar to oxidise?

_____

c) Is it possible for the green coating on the oxidised coins to change back to brown? Why/why not?

_____

_____

d) When the coating is rinsed off, what colour appears underneath? Why?

_____

_____

e) Circle the term that best represents the definition of oxidation.

   i) changing from brown to green

   ii) combining with oxygen in a chemical reaction

   iii) a change of energy in a substance

   iv) allowing substances to react over time

[7]

4. Two chemicals are poured into a bowl and an exothermic reaction results, as shown below.

a) What change will be seen in the thermometer? _____

[1]

b) About what temperature do you think it will be, and why? _____

_____

[2]

c) An exothermic reaction is defined as a reaction where energy is:

   i) absorbed   **ii)** released   **iii)** multiplied   **iv)** divided

[1]

d) Where does the energy come from? _____

[1]

4.4   Comparing physical and chemical changes (1)

1. Write whether the following are PHYSICAL (P) or CHEMICAL (C) changes.

a) frying an egg _____   b) mixing salt and water _____

c) mixing oil and water _____   d) burning leaves _____

e) a rusting bicycle _____   f) bleaching your hair _____

g) crushing a can _____   h) squeezing oranges for juice _____

[8]

2 Circle the correct answer.

a) Which shows that a chemical change is occurring?

    i) mixing sugar with oil   **ii)** adding vinegar to water

    iii) stirring sugar in juice   **iv)** souring of milk to make yoghurt

b) Which indicates a chemical change?

    i) fruits decaying   **ii)** clipping nails

    iii) water freezing   **iv)** shredding paper

c) A new chemical substance is formed when:

    i) plastic tears   **ii)** wood breaks

    iii) candles burn   **iv)** wire bends

[3]

3 Write whether the statements are TRUE or FALSE.

a) Bubbles exiting soda when the bottle is opened is a chemical change.

_____

b) Mechanical digestion by the teeth is a chemical change. _____

c) Rust is a new substance formed from iron. _____

d) Some physical changes may form a new substance. _____

e) An example of a chemical change occurs when water freezes. _____

[5]

4.5 Comparing physical and chemical changes (2)

1 A chemical change is the process by which one substance is changed into another substance. A chemical property is a feature of a substance that is observed during a chemical change.

Write in the columns to show whether the following are properties or changes, and whether these are physical or chemical.

BEHAVIOUR OR CHARACTERISTIC	PROPERTY OR CHANGE	CHEMICAL OR PHYSICAL
Melting point of water is 0° Celsius		
Ability to rust		
Volume of a stone		
Vitamin C tablets fizzing in water		
Boiling some water		
Acidity		
Heating soil		
Striking a match		

[8]

2 Write whether the statements are TRUE or FALSE.

a) In a physical combination of substances, each component can be identified.

_____

b) Most physical combinations can be separated by a magnet. _____

c) Most physical changes produce new substances. _____

d) It is difficult to separate physical combinations. _____

e) During chemical changes, substances may split and regroup. _____

[5]

4.6 Chemical reaction

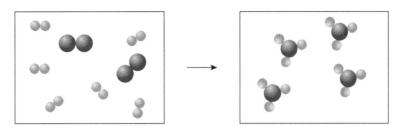

1 Explain what happens as the chemical reaction above occurs.

_____

_____

[1]

2 In every chemical reaction there are reactants and products. Complete these sentences.

a) Reactants are _____.

b) Products are _____.

[2]

3 When different atoms bond in a reaction, they form a new product known as a

_____.

[1]

4 For each of the following reactions, identify the atoms taking part in the reaction.

a) $2H_2 + O_2 \rightarrow 2H_2O$ _____

b) $Na + Cl \rightarrow NaCl$ _____

c) $Fe + S \rightarrow FeS$ _____

d) $Mg + 2F \rightarrow MgF_2$ _____

[8]

5 The table below shows models of the result of a physical combination and a chemical combination.

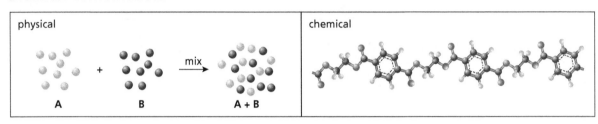

Identify TWO differences that you can see between the two combinations.

a) _____

_____

b) _____

_____

[2]

6 Juice is made from a physical combination while water is made from a chemical combination. Explain why there is a difference between the two combinations.

_____

_____

_____

[2]

7 Below are some atoms. Give the names of TWO combinations that may be made from the atoms.

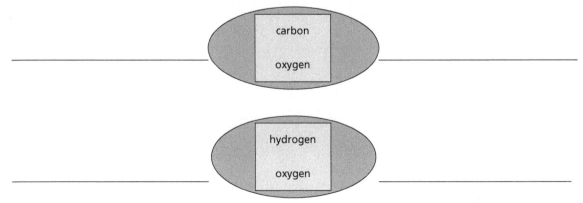

[4]

4.7 Types of chemical reaction

1 Combustion is also known as _____.

[1]

2 For combustion to occur, the fire needs fuel, heat and _____.

[1]

3 Look at the following pictures. Say what should be done to extinguish the flames in each case.

a)

_____

_____

_____

b)

_____

c)

_____

_____

[3]

4 Chemical decomposition is defined as _____

_____.

[1]

5 Some ammonium chloride crystals were dissolved in water and the solution formed became very cold.

Say whether a physical or a chemical reaction has occurred and explain your answer. _____

_____

[1]

6 Circle the correct answer.

a) Which of the following shows decomposition?

   i) $2HgO \rightarrow 2Hg + O_2$ **ii)** $2Mg + O_2 \rightarrow 2MgO$

   iii) $PbO + Ca \rightarrow CaO + Pb$ **iv)** $Fe + S \rightarrow FeS$

b) When water decomposes, $2H_2O \rightarrow 2H_2 + O_2$, what substances are formed?

   i)   oxygen as a liquid and hydrogen as a gas

   ii) both oxygen and hydrogen as liquids

   iii) oxygen as a gas and hydrogen as a liquid

   iv) both oxygen and hydrogen as gases

c) The results of chemical reactions are shown in the table below.

REACTION	OBSERVATION
X	Test tube became cold
Y	Test tube became warm

What conclusion can be drawn from the experiment?

   i)   X was endothermic.

   ii) Y was endothermic.

   iii) X was exothermic and Y was endothermic.

   iv) Both X and Y occurred on a hot day.

d) Which of the following statements about combustion reactions is false?

   i)   Combustion is the same as burning.

   ii) Oxygen is needed for combustion.

   iii) Combustion must be fuelled.

   iv) Heat is not necessarily needed.

e) Which of the following statements about a decomposition reaction is true?

   i)   There is only one reactant and one product.

   ii) There are two reactants and one product.

   iii) There is one reactant and two products.

   iv) Decomposition is the same as combustion.   **[5]**

4.8 Everyday chemical changes

1 Numerous chemical changes occur all the time, inside us and in the environment around us. In the table below, name FOUR useful changes and FOUR unwanted changes that occur.

	USEFUL CHANGES	UNWANTED CHANGES
a)		
b)		
c)		
d)		

[8]

2 Name FOUR chemical changes that occur in our bodies all the time.

a) _____

b) _____

c) _____

d) _____

[4]

3 Circle the correct answer.

a) All of the following indicate a chemical change, except for one. Which one?

i) colour change   ii) shape change

iii) energy change   iv) odour change

b) All of the following temperature changes indicate a chemical change, except one. Which one?

i) temperature increase as fuel burns

ii) temperature increase as chemicals react

iii) temperature decrease as gases cool

iv) temperature change as charcoal glows

c) Why is food kept in a refrigerator?

i) The chemical reaction of bacteria is slowed down.

ii) Bacteria die in the cold.

iii) The refrigerator is specially made for keeping food.

iv) Reheated food tastes better.

[3]

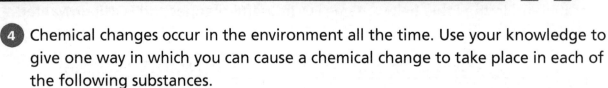

4 Chemical changes occur in the environment all the time. Use your knowledge to give one way in which you can cause a chemical change to take place in each of the following substances.

	SUBSTANCE	TO CAUSE CHEMICAL CHANGE
a)	Charcoal	
b)	Meat	
c)	Antacid tablets	
d)	Bread dough	
e)	Iron nails	

[5]

4.9 Solutions

1 What is a mixture? _____

_____

[1]

2 Here are the parts of a liquid-based mixture where dissolving occurs. Identify the parts.

_____   +   _____   →   _____

[3]

3 When more crystals are added to a solution, the dissolving time increases

because _____.

[1]

4 A solution is _____.

[1]

5 Write whether each of the following statements is TRUE or FALSE.

a) All solutions are mixtures. _____

b) All liquids can be mixed to create solutions. _____

c) Insoluble means that two substances can dissolve in one another. _____

d) Solutions with low concentrations are dilute. _____

e) An example of a solution is sugar and salt. _____

[5]

6 Use the clues below to complete the crossword puzzle about mixtures.

Across
4. mixture that is water based
5. physical combination of substances
6. substances seem to disappear in a liquid
8. liquid that dissolves a substance

Down
1. mixture with dissolved substances
2. having the ability to dissolve
3. uniform mixture of substances
7. solid that dissolves in a liquid

[5]

4.10   Dissolving

1 As more solute is dissolved in a solution, it becomes more _____.

[1]

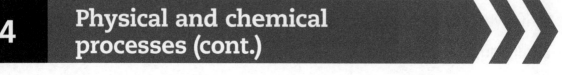

2 Below are four different volumes of water and a different mass of solute to be placed in each.

| 30 g | 13 g | 1.4 g | 24 g |

W   X   Y   Z

Using the formula shown below, find the concentration of each solution and place them in order from most dilute to most concentrated.

$$\frac{\text{Mass of solute (g)}}{\text{Volume of water (cm}^3)}$$

Order of concentrations

W _____

X _____

Y _____

Z _____

Show working in this space

[8]

4.11   Saturated solutions

1 What is a saturated solution?

_____

[1]

2 A solution is saturated at room temperature. What happens to its solubility level when it is heated?

_____

[1]

3 When a solution is heated, the space between its particles _____.

[1]

4 When a saturated solution is heated, it can _____ more crystals.

[1]

5 Circle the correct answer.

a) A solution containing less than the maximum possible amount of dissolved solute is:

i) saturated   **ii)** unsaturated   **iii)** dilute   **iv)** supersaturated

b) If a solution dissolves the maximum possible amount of solute, it is:

i) saturated   **ii)** unsaturated   **iii)** concentrated   **iv)** supersaturated

c) 100 cm^3 of water can dissolve 15 g of solute. If 25 g is dissolved in 250 cm^3 of water, then the 250 cm^3 of water is:

i) saturated   **ii)** unsaturated   **iii)** concentrated   **iv)** supersaturated

d) Solubility refers to the maximum _____ of solute dissolved in a given volume of solvent at a given temperature.

i) volume   **ii)** proportion   **iii)** mass   **iv)** ratio

[4]

4.12   Supersaturated solutions

1 The four illustrations above are referred to as crystals. Write TWO properties of crystals that they have in common.

a) _____

b) _____

[2]

2 Circle the correct answer.

a) The process by which a dissolved solute becomes solid again is called:

i) solidification   **ii)** deposition   **iii)** recrystallisation   **iv)** salvation

b) A solution whose concentration level is equal to its solubility level is:

i) unsaturated   **ii)** saturated   **iii)** soluble   **iv)** a crystal

c) In which situation are you least likely to get crystal growth?

i) room temperature too high   **ii)** solution is saturated

iii) room temperature too low   **iv)** solution is over-saturated

[3]

3 Write whether the following statements are TRUE or FALSE.

	STATEMENT	TRUE/FALSE
a)	Water is the best solvent for all crystals.	
b)	Crystallisation occurs when seawater evaporates.	
c)	Crystallisation is a physical change.	
d)	When evaporation occurs, the solvent crystallises as it returns to a liquid.	
e)	An important step in crystallisation is dissolving the solute in maximum amount of solvent.	
f)	A sugar solution becomes more concentrated because more solvent is added and crystallisation occurs.	

[6]

4.13 Mixtures

1 Circle the correct answer.

a) The difference between solutions and colloids is:

i) solubility   **ii)** reactivity

iii) size of particles   **iv)** temperature

b) All of these are mixtures except for one. Which one?

i) colloid   **ii)** suspension   **iii)** solution   **iv)** compound

c) A homogeneous mixture where particles do not dissolve in a liquid is called:

i) a colloid   **ii)** a solution   **iii)** an element   **iv)** a compound

[3]

2 Find the words about mixtures and solutions in the wordsearch below.

T	V	Y	L	N	J	F	D	K	N	R	S	J	Z	P	G	N
R	G	H	C	O	N	C	E	N	T	R	A	T	E	D	Z	A
V	H	O	G	X	O	C	O	Y	Q	X	S	D	I	L	U	J
D	P	M	Z	G	H	H	R	X	I	S	Z	N	Y	N	W	P
E	G	O	W	S	Z	S	B	Y	Y	U	T	W	R	X	Y	N
T	L	G	B	T	U	P	O	T	S	E	N	M	P	T	Z	S
A	H	E	S	J	N	O	Q	L	R	T	I	I	I	L	O	K
R	O	N	R	P	W	U	E	M	V	X	A	L	F	L	D	M
U	T	E	O	J	N	Z	I	U	T	E	I	L	U	O	C	C
T	W	O	S	E	Y	N	N	U	Q	B	N	T	M	U	R	X
A	L	U	U	N	G	K	R	C	U	A	E	T	Z	Q	X	M
S	Z	S	H	L	E	E	I	L	F	O	O	I	B	I	O	B
L	V	N	I	V	P	N	O	I	T	A	N	I	B	M	O	C
Z	R	N	O	D	W	S	D	I	S	S	O	L	V	E	R	B
B	G	E	R	U	T	A	R	E	P	M	E	T	K	M	W	J
Q	E	S	O	L	U	T	I	O	N	K	A	P	Y	E	O	W
W	O	O	P	M	O	L	E	C	U	L	E	S	X	T	I	T

AQUEOUS	COMBINATION	CONCENTRATED	CRYSTAL
DISSOLVE	HOMOGENEOUS	INTERMINGLING	MIXTURE
MOLECULES	SATURATED	SOLUBILITY	SOLUTE
SOLUTION	SOLVENT	TEMPERATURE	UNIFORM

[9]

3 Place a tick in the appropriate column to show whether each mixture is homogeneous or heterogeneous.

	MIXTURE	HOMOGENEOUS	HETEROGENEOUS
a)	Tap water		
b)	Chalky water		
c)	Muddy water		
d)	Milk		
e)	Guava nectar		
f)	Vinegar		

[6]

4 Write whether each of the statements is TRUE or FALSE.

a) Both emulsions and foams are colloids. _____

b) Pastes and solutions are heterogeneous. _____

c) Mixtures can be either homogeneous or heterogeneous. _____

d) All colloids are mixtures. _____

[4]

4.14 Mixtures (2)

1 Coins are made from mixtures of metals. These mixtures are called _____.

[1]

2 Many non-breakable household materials such as bowls and basins are made from materials called _____.

[1]

3 Circle the correct answer.

a) Air is a mixture because:

    i) it can be separated into its particles   **ii)** it can contain dust particles

    iii) it is a uniform mixture of gases   **iv)** it is transparent

b) Smoke is a colloid of:

    i) solid and gas   **ii)** liquid and solid

    iii) liquid and liquid   **iv)** gas and gas

c) Gravel is made of:

    i) solids   **ii)** solid and gas

    iii) solid and liquid   **iv)** solids dissolved in solids

d) One property that makes a suspension different from a solution or a colloid is:

    i) a suspension is always made of a solid and a liquid

    ii) the particles of a suspension reflect light

    iii) settling occurs in a suspension

    iv) some suspensions may be clear

[4]

4 Find the non-liquid based mixtures in the wordsearch.

L	R	D	A	T	D	O	D	T	L	I	S
P	I	U	L	X	G	P	M	N	S	M	G
U	A	S	L	Y	D	B	W	T	T	Q	O
M	X	T	O	Q	F	T	Y	L	C	E	Z
I	C	D	Y	Y	R	R	S	L	L	J	F
C	F	G	A	R	O	X	O	C	X	K	I
E	F	L	C	F	V	U	R	E	M	L	Q
Q	C	U	O	D	D	X	Q	P	G	E	S
L	W	A	E	R	O	G	E	L	Q	V	M
E	M	W	R	I	S	S	L	N	J	A	O
S	C	I	T	S	A	L	P	G	U	R	K
R	Z	N	T	A	X	A	M	S	H	G	E

AEROGEL   AIR   ALLOY   CLAY

CLOUD   DUST   GRAVEL   PLASTICS

PUMICE   SILT   SMOKE   STYROFOAM

[6]

5.2   Separating mixtures

1 How would you define separation of components in a mixture? _____

_____

[1]

2 Below are three methods of separation. Write the name of each method.

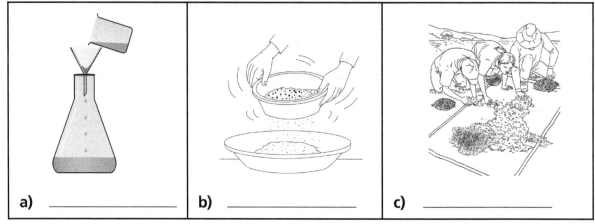

a) _____   b) _____   c) _____

[3]

3 State whether the method of separation for each of the following is HAND-PICKING, FILTRATION or SIEVING.

a) a mixture of rice and gravy _____

b) an assortment of sweets _____

c) chalk in water _____

d) various buttons _____

e) raisins and branflakes _____

f) powder and beads _____

[6]

4 Look at the diagram showing filtration and complete the sentence below.

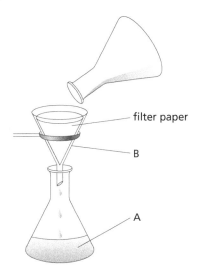

filter paper

B

A

The liquid (A) collected after filtration is called the _____ and the solid remaining on the filter paper (B) is the _____.

[2]

5 Circle the correct answer.

a) All of the following work by using a separation method, except for one. Which one?

i) fishing net   ii) fishnet tights   iii) tea strainer   iv) surgical mask

b) Hand-picking is a useful separation method for all of the following, except one. Which one?

i) sharpeners and erasers   ii) pieces of iron and copper
iii) rice and peas   iv) nails and screws

c) Filtration is recommended for separating all of the following mixtures, except for one. Which one?

i) impurities in water   ii) salt and soil
iii) sugar and sand   iv) syrup and molasses

[3]

5.3 and 5.4   Evaporation and distillation

1 What is evaporation? _____

_____

[1]

2 Circle the correct answer.

   a) All the following are examples of evaporation except for one. Which one?

      i)   the formation of bubbles as water boils

      ii) the sun drying a wet yard

      iii) water forming on a bathroom mirror

      iv) clothes drying on a washing line

   b) The disadvantage of evaporation is that:

      i)   all the solute is recovered   **ii)** the solute is called residue

      iii) the solvent evaporates   **iv)** the solvent cannot be recovered

   c) It is possible to separate water and alcohol using distillation because of their difference in:

      i)   boiling temperatures   **ii)** boiling densities

      iii) melting points   **iv)** colour

   d) All of the following pieces of apparatus are needed to demonstrate evaporation in the laboratory, except for one. Which one?

      i)   water bath   **ii)** wire gauze   **iii)** Bunsen burner **iv)** filter funnel

[4]

3 Write whether each of the following is TRUE or FALSE.

   a) Evaporation is a physical change. _____

   b) The formation of dew is due to evaporation. _____

   c) Matter gets warmer because of evaporation. _____

   d) The water on high hilltops rises because of precipitation in the water cycle.

   _____

   e) BOTH evaporation and distillation are used for separating a salt solution.

   _____

[5]

4 Name the parts of the distillation apparatus indicated by the label lines.

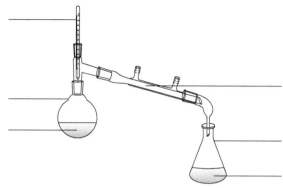

[6]

5 Some salt has fallen into sand. Explain what you would do to:

a) separate the two components _____

_____

b) recover the dry salt _____

_____

[2]

6 Distillation involves both _____ and condensation.

[1]

5.5 Fractional distillation

1 What is fractional distillation used for? _____

_____

[1]

2 Circle the correct answer.

a) Which process must occur before heated crude oil goes to the fractionating column?

    i) condensation   **ii)** distillation   **iii)** evaporation   **iv)** melting

b) As each component of crude oil liquefies, _____ occurs.

    i) condensation   **ii)** distillation   **iii)** evaporation   **iv)** melting

c) As crude oil heats up, the various oils separate by:

    i) atoms   **ii)** fractions   **iii)** test tubes   **iv)** pipelines

d) The fractionating column is _____ at the top and

_____ at the bottom.

    i) cool / hot   **ii)** solid / liquid   **iii)** hot / cool   **iv)** liquid / solid

e) For diesel and petrol to be separated, they must both:

   i)   be liquids   **ii)**   be different colours

  iii) have different boiling points   **iv)** have different volume ranges

                                                                   [5]

3   Name the parts of the fractional distillation apparatus indicated by the labelling lines.

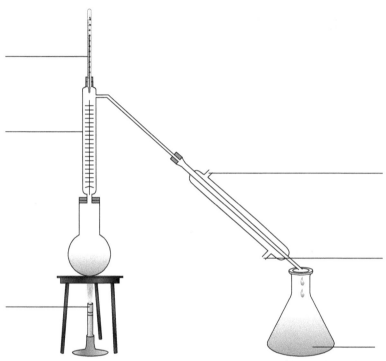

                                                                     [6]

5.6   Chromatography

1 What is chromatography? _____

_____

                                                                     [1]

2 State whether each of the statements on chromatography is TRUE or FALSE.

   a) Chromatography works because lots of water or alcohol is used. _____

   b) Chromatography depends on the speed at which dye moves. _____

   c) Alcohol is able to dissolve ink. _____

   d) Darker-coloured markers contain fewer dyes than lighter colours. _____

e) When alcohol is used in chromatography, it must be covered to reduce the evaporation rate of the alcohol. _____

f) In paper chromatography, the inks are absorbed by the paper. _____

g) Gases are used as a medium in chromatography. _____

[7]

3 The diagram below shows chromatography occurring. Circle ALL the possible substances 'A' could be.

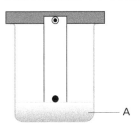

solvent	liquid	acid
filtrate	water	alcohol

A

[3]

5.7 and 5.8   Other methods of separating mixtures

1 Circle the correct answer.

a) The purpose of sedimentation is to:

   i)   increase alkalinity of water
   ii) decrease the bacteria in water
   iii) improve the volume of oxygen in water
   iv) decrease the solids in water

b) The factor that does not affect sedimentation is:

   i)   particle size   **ii)** particle density
   iii) water temperature   **iv)** reservoir altitude

c) The purpose of decanting is to allow:

   i)   acidity to be separated from wine
   ii) wine to be identified
   iii) clear wine to separate from its sediment
   iv) various wines to separate

d) The water is squeezed out of clothes in a washing machine using:

   i) centrifugation **ii)** filter funnel   **iii)** separating funnel **iv)** evaporation

e) Immiscible liquids may be separated by using:

   i) a Liebig condenser   **ii)** an evaporating dish

   iii) a separating funnel   **iv)** a filter funnel

f) Which method cannot be used to separate sand and water?

   i) decanting   **ii)** evaporation

   iii) separating funnel   **iv)** filtration

g) The sedimentation process _____ suspended matter.

   i) clumps up   **ii)** settles   **iii)** filters   **iv)** colours

h) When cream is churned at dairies to make butter, the buttermilk is separated from the butter using the process of:

   i) decanting   **ii)** evaporation   **iii)** separating funnel   **iv)** filtration

i) _____ is quicker but less effective than filtration.

   i) Decanting   **ii)** Centrifuging   **iii)** Crystallisation   **iv)** Distillation

j) Solids that can settle are removed by:

   i) turbulence   **ii)** oxidation   **iii)** gravity   **iv)** filtration

k) _____ is used in laboratories for separating blood and urine.

   i) Filtration   **ii)** Crystallisation   **iii)** Centrifugation   **iv)** Decanting

l) Which diagram shows decanting apparatus?

   i)   **ii)**   **iii)**   **iv)**

gauze
tripod
Bunsen
burner

[12]

6.2 Speed

1 Define speed. _____

_____

[1]

2 Calculate each of the following and write your answers in the right-hand columns.

a)	A car travels for four hours and it covers a distance of 50 km each hour. How many km does it cover for the four hours?		

b)	A swimmer covers 180 m in 20 seconds. How many metres does she swim in one second?		

c)	A fisherman travels between two islands, covering a distance of 210 km at a rate of 35 km every hour. How many hours does his journey last?	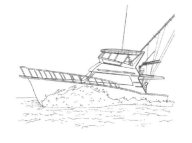	

[6]

6 Motion (cont.)

6.3 Relationship between speed, distance and time

1 Below is a diagram showing the relationship between speed, distance and time.

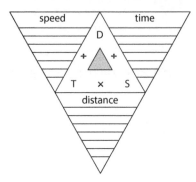

Use the diagram to complete the following equations:

a) SPEED =   **b)** DISTANCE =   **c)** TIME =

[3]

2 Use the formulae above to work out the following. Remember, km per hr; m per s. (Show all your working.)

a) A motorist completes a journey in 45 minutes, covering a distance of 75 km. At what speed did he travel?

b) A train left Weston and arrived at Easton 3 hours and 30 minutes later. The speed was 104 km per hour. What was the total distance covered?

c) Ellie ran 6 km in 30 minutes. What was her speed in:

i) km per hr?   **ii)** m per s?

d) Find the time in hours and minutes that it took a cyclist to ride a distance of 45 km at a rate of 12 km per hour.

e) Jan cycled 30 km from school to home at an average speed of 12 km per hour. If she left school at 3:00 p.m., at what time did she arrive home?

[10]

6.4 Distance–time graphs

1 The distance–time graphs below show the journey of a pair of twins from their home to the cinema. Examine the graph and answer the questions following.

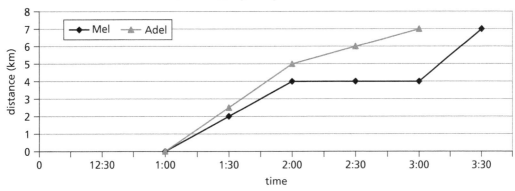

a) How far is the cinema from their home? _____

[1]

b) At what time did the twins arrive at the cinema? _____

[1]

c) What was their speed for the first hour?

  i) Mel _____   **ii)** Adel _____

[2]

d) What does the horizontal part of the graph show? _____

[1]

e) At what time were the twins 2 km apart? _____

[1]

f) When Adel arrived, how far behind was Mel? _____

[1]

g) What was each twin's average speed for the whole journey?

  i) Mel _____   **ii)** Adel _____

[2]

6.5 and 6.6   Displacement, velocity and acceleration

1 Circle the correct answer in the right-hand column.

a)	The unit of speed is...	m/s	s/g
		hr/s	kg/m
b)	While _____ gives how fast a vehicle is travelling, _____ tells both how fast and its direction.	speed/velocity	rate/speed
		rate/velocity	speed/ acceleration
c)	Which is a measure of velocity?	50 North	50 m
		50 m/s	50 m/s, East
d)	If a stone is falling at 5 m/s for 15 s, we can calculate its...	velocity	speed
		direction	distance
e)	What distance will you cover by travelling 9 m/s for 2 minutes?	18 km	1.8 km
		1080 m	10.8 km
f)	The rate at which velocity changes is...	speed	acceleration
		direction	time
g)	A car going at 25 m/s changes to 0 m/s. This means that it has...	slowed down	lost direction
		stopped	lost brakes
h)	A van can change from rest to 40 m/s in 8 seconds. What is its acceleration?	5 m/s in 1 minute	5 m/s in 1 second
		8 m in 1 second	40 m in 8s

[8]

2 Write whether the statements are TRUE or FALSE.

a) Speed is velocity with a given direction. _____

b) The speed of an aeroplane is given as 400 km/h. _____

c) The acceleration of a car is given as 80 km/h to the South. _____

d) Distance divided by time is velocity. _____

e) Acceleration is change of velocity with time. _____

[5]

6.7–6.10 Newton's laws

1 Circle the correct answer.

a) Newton's _____ law refers to action/reaction.

     i) first   **ii)** second   **iii)** third

b) Newton's _____ law refers to the law of inertia.

     i) first   **ii)** second   **iii)** third

c) Which of Newton's laws relates force to acceleration?

     i) first   **ii)** second   **iii)** third

d) If no outside force is applied, an object at rest will:

     i) stay at rest   **ii)** increase velocity   **iii)** decrease mass

e) Newton's second law is based on the formula:

     i) $E = mc^2$ **ii)** $A = pr^2$ **iii)** $F = ma$

f) Define inertia.

     i) a force opposing gravity   **ii)** the mass of an object
     iii) the tendency to continue in a state of uniform motion

                                                                                 [6]

2 Write whether the statements are TRUE or FALSE.

a) Newton's first law explains why seatbelts are worn. _____

b) Inertia depends on the mass of an object. _____

c) Momentum is explained by Newton's third law. _____

d) Acceleration occurs when forces are balanced. _____

                                                                                             [4]

6.11–6.13   The turning effect of a force

1 Circle the correct answer.

a) The moment of a force will cause an object to go:

   i) backwards   **ii)** sideways   **iii)** downwards   **iv)** around

b) Tim, weighing 350 N, sits 3.5 m from the fulcrum of a seesaw while Tom, weighing 400 N, sits 2 m from the fulcrum. Which boy will go down?

   i) Tim   **ii)** Tom   **iii)** both   **iv)** neither

c) To loosen a nut easily, a _____ is needed.

   i) short spanner with its large turning effect
   ii) short spanner with a large force
   iii) a heavy spanner with a larger force
   iv) long spanner with its large turning effect

d) What force (F) is needed to balance the bar below?

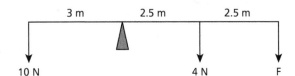

   i) 20 N   **ii)** 10 N
   iii) 6 N   **iv)** 8 N

[4]

2 Write whether the statements are TRUE or FALSE.

a) The two types of moment of force are clockwise and anticlockwise.

_____

b) The SI unit for moment of force is N m. _____

c) Turning effect of force is also known as torque. _____

d) A body in dynamic equilibrium is in uniform motion along a straight line.

_____

e) Moment of force is defined as F + d. _____

[5]

6.14 Levers

1 Levers are classified as _____.

[1]

2 How many orders of levers are there? _____

[1]

3 To which order does each of the following levers belong?

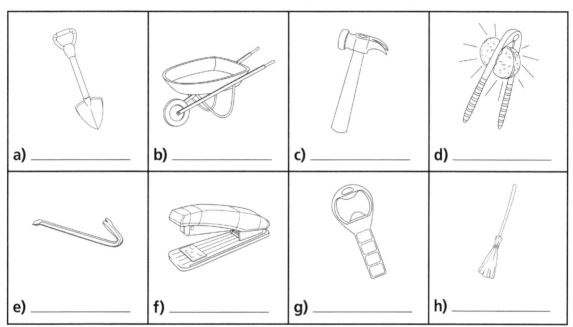

a) _____ b) _____ c) _____ d) _____

e) _____ f) _____ g) _____ h) _____

[4]

4 Circle the correct answer.

a) The lever pivots on its:

i) arm **ii)** fulcrum **iii)** end **iv)** middle

b) In the middle of the second-class lever is the:

i) input force **ii)** output force **iii)** fulcrum **iv)** effort

c) A racing car is levered up so that the tyres can be changed. Which part of the lever system is the racing car?

i) effort **ii)** fulcrum **iii)** load **iv)** mass

[3]

6 Motion (cont.)

6.15 Calculations on levers

1 The seesaw on the right is not balanced. Give THREE adjustments that could be made to balance the seesaw.

a) _____

[1]

b) _____

[1]

c) _____

[1]

2 Look at the diagram and solve the problem.

What weight should be at X so that the figure on the right would be balanced?

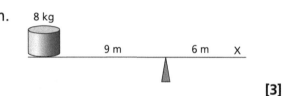

[3]

3 Gabi and Tyna are seated on either side of a seesaw. Gabi, sitting 4 m from the fulcrum, weighs 60 kg and Tyna weighs 45 kg. How far from the fulcrum should Tyna sit so that the seesaw is balanced?

[3]

6.16–6.18 Centre of gravity, stability and equilibrium

1 Circle the correct answer.

a) When a cricket ball is hit outside the centre of gravity (cg) of a bat, the ball will:

   i)   go to the boundary   ii)   travel very far

   iii) spin rapidly   iv) travel less far than if hit at cg

b) Which is TRUE about gravity?

   i)   It acts through air but not through water or land.

   ii) It cannot affect high-flying aeroplanes.

   iii) It always pulls towards Earth's centre.

   iv) It has the same force all over the Earth.

c) A metre rule is balanced when pivoted at 50 cm because:

    i) the force acting against it is 0

    ii) there is equal distance on both sides

    iii) weight cannot affect it

    iv) both sides are equal in length and force

d) A body's weight tends to work through a single point referred to as the:

    i) moment   **ii)** centre of gravity

    iii) fixed point   **iv)** fulcrum

e) If gravity pulls things towards the centre of the Earth, why don't we all go through the ground?

    i) Gravity doesn't act below the ground.

    ii) The ground exerts an equal force upwards.

    iii) Gravity runs out.

    iv) The ground is much too compact.

f) An object will not be balanced when:

    i) the centre of gravity is directly over the point of support

    ii) there is a high centre of gravity and a narrow base

    iii) both clockwise and anticlockwise moments are equal

    iv) there is no torque

g) The centre of gravity is located where _____ is concentrated.

    i) more weight   **ii)** less weight

    iii) more mass   **iv)** less mass

h) The ability of an object to maintain its balance after being disturbed is called:

    i) equality   **ii)** sturdiness   **iii)** equilibrium   **iv)** stability

i) The four vessels are the same height. Which is most stable?

    i)   **ii)**   **iii)**   **iv)**

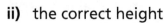

j) The Tower of Pisa in Italy is tilted but does not topple over because it is:

    i) stable   **ii)** the correct height

    iii) a counterweight   **iv)** a gravity centre

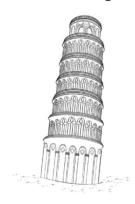

[10]

2 Write whether the statements are TRUE or FALSE.

a) As an object falls, air resistance acts in the opposite direction to its movement.

_____

b) Both friction and weight are affected by gravity. _____

c) An object suspended in water feels heavier than if it is suspended in air.

_____

d) A moving object eventually slows down because it runs out of force.

_____

e) When a beam is balanced, its weight cannot cause a turning effect.

_____

f) Two forces will be in equilibration only if a third force acts against them.

_____

g) If two forces are opposing each other, it is not possible to have balance.

_____

h) When compared with the Moon, you feel heavier on Earth because gravity is bigger on Earth. _____

[8]

7 Thermal energy

7.2 Heat and temperature

1 Heat is defined as _____

_____.

[1]

2 Just like any form of energy, heat is measured in units of _____.

[1]

3 Circle the correct answer.

a) Whenever there is a temperature change, which of the following is TRUE about energy?

   i) Cold moves to warmer regions.

   ii) Warm moves to cooler regions.

   iii) Energy moves slowly.

   iv) Energy moves rapidly.

b) The transfer of heat energy is complete:

   i) when both objects have the same temperature

   ii) when the heat energy reaches its boiling point

   iii) when the amount of energy is the same

   iv) heat transfer is never complete

c) A hot iron cools down because:

   i) the iron needs to be changed

   ii) the iron's energy is transferred to the room

   iii) the thermostat needs to be turned down

   iv) the room's temperature is transferred to the iron

[3]

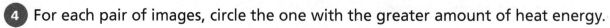

4 For each pair of images, circle the one with the greater amount of heat energy.

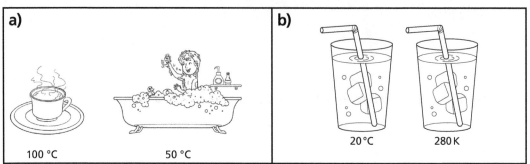

a)   b)

100 °C   50 °C

20 °C   280 K

[2]

7.3   Thermometers

1 Look at the liquid-in-glass thermometer below.

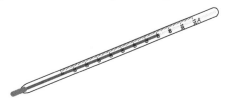

a) Give TWO features of the thermometer.

i) _____   ii) _____

[2]

b) Explain the importance of each feature.

i) _____

[1]

ii) _____

[1]

2 Circle the correct answer.

a) Temperature is measured in:

    i) degrees Celsius   **ii)** degrees kelvin
    iii) degrees   **iv)** Fahrenheit

b) Absolute zero is:

   i) 273 K   **ii)** 0 °C

   iii) −273 °C   **iv)** 0 °F

c) Which two temperature scales have the same interval step size?

   i) Celsius and Fahrenheit

   ii) Celsius and kelvin

   iii) Fahrenheit and kelvin

   iv) Celsius and body temperature

[3]

7.4 Cooling graphs

1 Study the graph of cooling substance Z and answer the questions that follow.

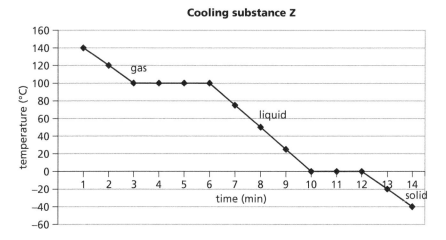

Cooling substance Z

a) At what time did Z begin condensing? _____

b) After how many minutes did Z begin to freeze? _____

c) What happened to Z from 3 to 6 minutes? _____

d) What was the temperature of Z after $2\frac{1}{2}$ minutes? _____

e) In what state would Z be at 160 °C? _____

f) After 14 minutes, what would be the state of Z? _____

g) For how long was all of Z in the liquid state? _____

[7]

7.5 and 7.6   Heat transfer: conduction and metals

1 What is conduction? _____

                                                               [1]

2 What type of materials are the best heat conductors?

_____

                                                               [1]

3 Metals do not all conduct heat at the same rate. The apparatus below shows five different metal prongs used to test for heat conductivity. Examine the apparatus and list THREE variables that must be controlled in order for the results to be correct.

a) _____

b) _____

c) _____

                                                               [3]

4 Examine the diagram below and explain what may have caused the two campers to have such different reactions to the same activity.

_____

_____

_____

_____

_____

                                                               [1]

5 You have a choice of three cups to put your hot tea in: metal, ceramic or plastic. Which would you choose and why?

_____

_____

_____

_____

[2]

7.7 and 7.8 Heat transfer – convection

1 What is convection? _____

[1]

2 In what states of matter does convection occur? _____

[1]

3 The diagram shows a bonfire. THREE major activities occur in the air around a bonfire.

a) Draw arrows on the diagram to show the effect of the heat on the surrounding air.

b) Indicate what is happening at the arrows. (For example, 'hot air rising'.)

[3]

4 The diagrams below show how land and sea breezes occur. Explain the reason for the direction of airflow in each.

a) Sea breeze _____

_____

_____

_____

_____

b) Land breeze _____

_____

_____

_____

_____

[4]

7.9 and 7.10   Heat transfer – radiation

1 What is radiation? _____

[1]

2 Complete the sentences to say whether the following are examples of CONDUCTION, CONVECTION or RADIATION.

a) Hot soup is stirred with a metal spoon. The spoon gets hot due to

_____.

b) A lamp with liquid has blobs that float and sink continually because of

_____.

c) Sammy stands close to a fireplace. Soon he becomes very hot because of

_____.

d) Air near the ceiling of a house is warmer because of _____.

e) Tyn burns rubbish. All the overhead wires in the garden get warped due to

_____.

[5]

7.11–7.13   Thermal insulators and conductors

1 Circle the correct answer in the right-hand column.

a)	Oven gloves are worn because they are...	i) made to keep your hands warm ii) good thermal insulators iii) cool and comfortable iv) good heat conductors
b)	The better heat conductor is a...	i) piece of wood ii) sheet of paper iii) copper rod iv) long black stick
c)	When ice cream is placed in a metal bowl...	i) warmth travels from bowl to ice cream ii) warmth travels from ice cream to bowl iii) cold travels from ice cream to bowl iv) cold travels from bowl to ice cream
d)	To keep the ice cream from melting quickly, place it in a _____ bowl with a _____ lid.	i) metal/metal ii) metal/plastic iii) plastic/plastic iv) ceramic/metal
e)	One disadvantage of using a metal spoon in a pan on the stove top is...	i) cold would travel to the food from the room and a longer time would be spent cooking ii) heat would travel from the boiling pot to your hand iii) metal spoons get rusty iv) metal spoons scratch the metal pan and the metal is added to your food

[5]

2 Write whether each of the following statements is TRUE or FALSE.

a) A flask can keep things hot on a cold day and cold on a hot day. _____

b) Normally materials that are poor conductors are poor insulators. _____

c) The transfer of heat energy by direct contact is convection. _____

d) Air is a poor heat conductor. _____

e) It is better to wear white on a cold day as it will absorb heat to keep you warm. _____

f) Liquids take a long time to cool as they conduct heat slowly. _____

[6]

8.2   What is an ecosystem?

1 What is ecology? _____

_____

[1]

2 The images below show two different environments. Draw the following on each image:

a) THREE living things that you would find if the environment were an ecosystem.

b) THREE non-living things that you would find if the environment were an ecosystem.

POND	TREE

[6]

3 Complete the statements so they are true.

a) Populations sharing the same environment form a/an _____.

[1]

b) Food, water, shelter and space make up the organism's _____.

[1]

c) A person who studies ecosystems is called a/an _____.

[1]

d) Population is defined as _____.

[1]

8.3 Creating an ecosystem

1 What is an ecosystem? _____

_____

[1]

2 Think of an ecosystem that you would like to create for your class to study. In the space provided below, draw what your ecosystem should look like.

[5]

3 Find the ten words associated with ecosystems in the wordsearch.

S	E	I	C	E	P	S	K	Z	M
B	M	M	X	C	H	L	G	Y	S
U	C	N	F	O	H	C	N	Y	I
P	O	P	U	L	A	T	I	O	N
P	C	I	T	O	I	B	V	N	A
U	B	I	R	G	N	I	I	R	G
S	U	R	V	I	V	A	L	B	R
U	W	U	W	S	Y	O	R	S	O
I	H	T	A	T	I	B	A	H	H
Y	T	I	N	U	M	M	O	C	W

biotic	community
ecologist	habitat
living	niche
organism	population
species	survival

[5]

8.4 Photosynthesis

1 The source of energy for all ecosystems is _____.

[1]

2 The diagram below shows a plant undergoing photosynthesis. For each arrow, say what is either absorbed or released by the plant.

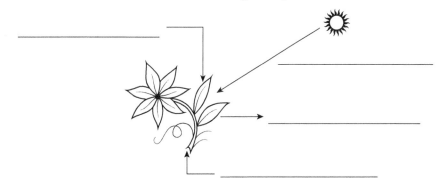

[4]

3 A plant was set up as shown in the apparatus below.

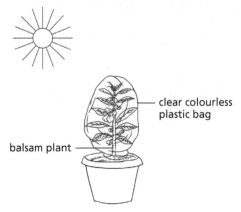

a) Would it be able to photosynthesise? _____

[1]

b) Give the reason to support your answer for a). _____

_____

_____

[2]

4 What food does the plant produce during photosynthesis? _____

[1]

5 Complete the following equation for the process of photosynthesis.

carbon dioxide + water   ⟶   _____ + _____

[2]

8.5   Producers, consumers and decomposers

1 Circle the correct answer.

a) What is a lettuce plant considered to be?

    i)   consumer   ii) producer   iii) decomposer   iv) vegetarian

b) If an organism ate a meat burger with lettuce, cheese and ketchup, that would make it:

    i)   a herbivore   ii) a carnivore   iii) a decomposer iv) an omnivore

c) Which of these is an example of a primary consumer?

    i)   fox   ii) caterpillar   iii) plant   iv) fish

d) All of these are decomposers except one. Which one?

    i) centipede   **ii)** fungus   **iii)** worm   **iv)** millipede

e) What makes a plant a producer?

    i) Plants supply food for the ecosystem.
    ii) Plants are produced from seeds.
    iii) Plants make their own food.
    iv) Plants can absorb both carbon dioxide and oxygen.

    [5]

2 Write whether the statements are TRUE or FALSE.

a) Fungi break down dead organisms so fungi are consumers in an ecosystem. _____

b) A worm is a secondary consumer. _____

c) All primary consumers eat plants. _____

d) Scavengers are secondary consumers. _____

e) Primary consumers are herbivores. _____

f) A carnivore hunts for its food. It is a predator. _____

    [6]

8.6 Food chains

1 What is a food chain? _____

_____

    [2]

2 Circle the correct answer.

a) Which part of the food chain is not affected by an animal becoming extinct?

    i) producers   **ii)** consumers   **iii)** predators   **iv)** humans

b) An example of a consumer eating another consumer is:

    i) a worm eating decaying grass   **ii)** a human eating salad
    iii) a bird eating bugs   **iv)** a Venus fly trap catching a fly

c) One of these is not a producer. Which one?

    i) gooseberry   **ii)** zebra grass   **iii)** catmint   **iv)** fungus

d) One of these is not a consumer. Which one?

i) moss   **ii)** mouse   **iii)** mole   **iv)** moose

[4]

3 Write which organism from the images fits each of the following descriptions.

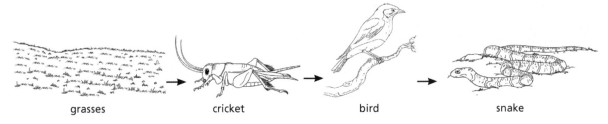

grasses   cricket   bird   snake

a) secondary consumer _____

b) predator _____

c) producer _____

d) prey _____

e) serpent _____

f) bamboo _____

[6]

8.7   Food webs

1 Examine the food chains in the table and answer the questions that follow.

FOOD CHAINS	
a) Grass → rabbit → owl	**f)** Grass → earthworm → shrew → owl
b) Grass → earthworm → owl	**g)** Plankton → shrimp → tuna → shark → human
c) Grass → human	**h)** Plankton → cod → seal → shark → cat
d) Grass → cow → human	**i)** Grass → earthworm → bird → cat → owl
e) Grass → zebra → human	**j)** Plankton → shrimp → bird → owl

a) In the space provided, create a food web from the food chains above.

[5]

b) From the food web above, write one organism for each description below.

i) omnivore _____

ii) land predator _____

iii) carnivore _____

iv) sea predator _____

v) herbivore _____

vi) air predator _____

[6]